BY-GONE BROCKEN

1.	Margaret Post's Brocken|	
2.	The Fire Bell	
3.	The War Memorial	5
4.	Brockenhurst Football Club	6
5.	Tommy Street Ironmonger	7
6.	Lowers Aimers - The Forest Park Hotel	8
7.	The Holt - Balmer Lawn Hotel	9
8.	The Christmas Turkey from Egg to Table	11
9.	Christmas Celebrations, 1927/8	12
10.	Electricity	14
11.	The Bailey Benefice (Trust)	15
12.	The Railway to Lymington	16
13.	Julia Margaret Cameron	17
14.	Marlpool House and Black Bridge	18
15.	When the School was the Community Hub	19
16.	The Bakehouse	20
17.	The Bells of St. Nicholas	20
18.	Pictures of Brockenhurst's 'Island'	22
	Location Map (*inside back cover*)	23

Author's store - Christmas 1989

1. Margaret Post's Brockenhurst Badger

The Badger symbol now used by the Village Hall and Parish Council and in various forms by organisations in the village was originally drawn by Margaret Post as a promotional symbol of the Hall Committee and reproduced on mugs for fund raising.

Margaret Post was a French mistress at the Grammar School but also had a talent for various forms of art. She helped produce props for the school plays; she made the Donkey's head for Bottom in 'A Midsummer Night's Dream' and, as a keen member of the W.I., she became involved in drama productions and the village pantomime.

As part of the 1979 Diamond Jubilee celebration of the Village Women's Institute she produced a collage. This is a tapestry map of the village surrounded by a collage depicting the shops and services that contributed to life in the village with photographs of the Parish Council, church Ministers, School masters, doctors, and others.

It is now stored at the Village Hall. *Logo reproduced with assistance from the Parish Council.*

2. The Fire Bell at Rosetta Cottage, Sway Road

In 1911 a fund was started to provide a village commemoration for King George V's Coronation. A fire bell, to summon the volunteer members of the newly formed Brockenhurst Fire Brigade, was the main item and £15 was allocated for it. The bell was erected on an oak post, donated by the Morant estate, in October 1912, in the grounds of Rosetta Cottage on Sway Road by the cross roads.

It was not until John Morant, then aged 5 years, rang it the first time on 23 July 1913 (due to a fortunate lack of fires) and the brigade members response was tested.

In January 1914 Brigade members complained that the new bell could not be heard at a sufficient distance away and requested that it be put on a higher post. The Parish Council considered this an unnecessary expense and declined to act, their point being that hearing the bell depended on the way of the wind. However, in 1928 it was re-erected on a taller post because the village had grown and it was no longer within hearing of all brigade members. At the same time new gallows were erected for the drying of the hoses.

The bell summoned the firemen until the brigade was taken over by the New Forest Rutal District Council in January 1939. In war-time they were summoned by other means but by 1946 the daytime call was sounded by the 'All Clear' siren with bells in their homes at night.

On Saturday 30th October 2004, the bell, after all the metal work had been cleaned and the post refurbished, was re-dedicated by the Hampshire Deputy Chief Fire Officer, Alan House, who was once a Brockenhurst part-time fireman.

Today the bell is rung to denote the beginning and end of the two minutes silence on Remembrance Sunday. Four plaques on the post relate to its history.

3. The War Memorial

The War Memorial stands on the site of the filled-in village pond where the cattle drank in summer and children skated in winter. In 1909, the Morant Trustees offered the site for a Parish Hall but the community rejected this as being unaffordable. It was also considered for a Parish office and Fire Brigade storage but this was objected to. The 1914-1918 war prompted the site's use for memorial.

In 1917 a brick built 'shrine' was erected, initially listing on paper the names of 249 local men serving in the Forces. Alongside were the names of those killed in the war and also of New Zealand soldiers who had died at the village's military hospital. It was enclosed with a gate and iron railings.

The dedication, on the 4 July 1917, (*pictured left*) was performed by Brockenhurst-born Rev. Frederick Bowden-Smith, with the vicar, Rev. Arthur Chambers, other church leaders, and hospital chaplains. Convalescing New Zealand Soldiers formed a guard of honour.

In June 1919, a hard wood board inscribed in gold lettering with the names of the Brockenhurst men 'who had fallen' was placed in the shrine and dedicated.

Finally, the War Memorial, an obelisk of Portland Stone, was erected in 1921 and unveiled by a local disabled ex-serviceman, 25 year old Cpl Frank Charles Perkins, on Sunday 26 June. The original bronze tablet on the front of the memorial contains 50 names.

After the War Memorial was erected, the wooden board and roll of names was put in the porch of St. Nicolas' Church, where it remains, with the addition of the names of those who fell in the 1939-45 war.

On Remembrance Sunday 1948 Vice Admiral Sir Geoffrey Blake unveiled another tablet, on the north side of the War Memorial, to commemorate those who fell in the Second World War. This tablet lists 29 names.

William Mutter of Latchmere House provided a path from the road to the memorial in 1956 and later the family donated two seats in memory of their son, Lt. Ronald Mutter, who was killed in Germany on 27 April 1945, just ten days before the Second World War ended.

The surrounding iron railings were removed and the complete site fenced in the 1980's. A third tablet was added in 2002, on the south side, with 26 names that had been missed from the 1914-18 list and 2 from the 1939-45. It also records another serviceman, Capt. Nigel Sutton, killed while serving in in Northern Ireland in 1973, and also the names of 9 local civilian war casualties. The 2002 list was the result of extensive research by villager John Cockram for his book 'Brockenhurst and the Two World Wars'.

(Frank Perkins, of Partridge Road, had been an apprentice at the International Stores prior to enlisting. His disability, of the loss of a leg, prevented him from returning to shop work so he took a clerical post. During the second World War he was the quartermaster Sargent for the Home Guard, and awarded the M.B.E. in 1958)

4. The Brockenhurst Football Club

The Brockenhurst Football Club was founded in 1898 and their first pitch was behind the Baptist Chapel on Lyndhurst Road. However few village groups had such a long journey to their present home!

After Lyndhurst Road, the club moved to a field in Wide Lane (Sway Road), then after the First World War to the Polo Field (now College grounds). In the late 1920's they moved to Fathers Field until 1931 when the land was needed to build the Council houses. The club moved to a field at Black Knoll House, but this required moving play to the open forest towards the end of each season to allow the grass to recover. From 1934 until the end of WW2 the Club moved to Oberfield in Rhinefield Road. 1946 saw another move to the County Council land at Tile Barn hill.

On purchasing the land from the Estate, for £630, the Football Club moved to Grigg Lane in May 1950. Prior to 1940, this was a playing field for the Church of England School. If the Parish Council had managed to obtain a grant from the Playing Fields Association it would have been the village recreation ground.

The 1950 purchase included the present ground and land adjoining Fathers Field which the Club then sold to the New Forest Rural District Council, for £456, to enable the building of the newer houses in Fathers Field and Horlock Road. The proceeds were used to provide a well-drained pitch and other facilities.

Tree felling at the Football Club in 1952

The draining of the ground involved diverting a ditch for 40 yards and, in forest tradition this had been lined with a row of large oak trees, which later needed to be felled to provide room for a club house and stand.

The Supporters Club raised the funds for the materials to enable club members to provide the labour by the beginning of May 1952. Twenty years later, in 1972, a thriving Social Club was established.

Excavations for a new stand commenced in 1975 and it was formally opened on 23 August 1977 with seating for 200 people, above the two changing rooms for the teams, equipped with showers.

The club was a founding member of the New Forest league.

5. Thomas 'Tommy' Street, Farrier and Ironmonger

Thomas Street was a farrier and blacksmith who had a forge in Balmer Lawn Road. The site was opposite Lunn Brothers saw mill behind the Balmer Lawn Hotel, which processed timber brought from surrounding woodlands on lumber waggons hauled by up to six heavy shire horses. The forge shoed the horses and made and repaired forestry tools. Today the site is housing.

In 1914 Mr. P.A. Pope, the blacksmith on the Island site, retired and Thomas Street took it over (see page 22 for pictures). In 1915 the Masters family, which had owned the site for some 400 years, decided to demolish it and build Brockenhurst Chambers (Island shop). Mr Street moved to a new forge in Brookley Road, next to the Foresters Arms. He started selling general ironmongery when Arthur Keeping vacated his workshop on the site and moved to 'Surrey Lodge' in Meerut Road.

 The Masters family also owned the land opposite, from Cherry Tree Cottage to Lloyds Bank. They built the 'Red House' (Warwick Lodge) and intended a row of shops. But by 1927 only one was completed, to which Tommy Street and his wife moved the business, and this is today's 'Streets'.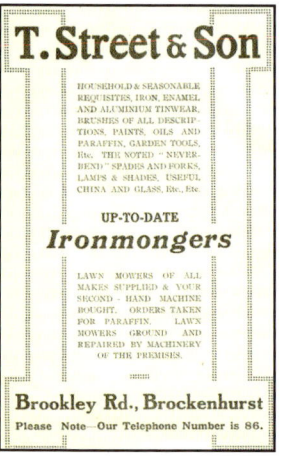

Mr. & Mrs Street, the 'up-to-date' ironmongers (*shown above*), retired in 1955 and sold the business to Harold Bush and upon his death it was enlarged by his son Eric.

Alan Bartlett, who with his wife Alison (and formerly brother and sister-in-law David and Evelyn) has run Streets since 1995, assisted Eric Bush as a 'Saturday lad'. His family in Brockenhurst dates from before 1800. His grandfather, Harold, was a prominent member of the Brockenhurst Band in the 20's and 30's, and a supporter of the Football Club's ground development in the 1950's.

6. Lower Aimers - The Forest Park Hotel

In 1862 the Rev. John Falls was the first vicar when Brockenhurst church ceased to be a chapel of Boldre and the property known as Setley Brake East and West in Vicarage Lane (Tile Barn Lane), was built as the vicarage.

A new vicarage was built in 1879 on land known as 'Lower Aimers' on Ober Farm (Rhinefield) Road. The original building now forms the main entrance and central part of the Forest Park Hotel. It was then standing in a considerable acreage of surrounding land and the income from the fields was part of the vicar's stipend. Sunday School children enjoyed their annual treats here of games and sports with a provided picnic but they had to bring their own mugs.

The Revd. Rupert Pain was resident, before leaving the parish in 1899 and the Rev. Arthur Chambers occupied it for a very short time until moving to 'The Old Vicarage' (as it is now known) which was built on the development of surrounding land, Forest Park Road.

Lower Aimers was sold in 1903 to the Hayden family, who were the owners of the Branksome Towers Hotel at Bournemouth. It was extended and opened as The Forest Park Hotel. Advertisements for these two hotels were prominent on the smithy at the Island before the building of Brockenhurst Chambers in 1915.

In 1914 the hotel was requisitioned by the military for an annex to the Lady Hardinge Hospital of the 3rd Lahore and 7th Meerut divisions of the Indian Army on Tile Barn Hill. A crematorium was built to observe the rites of those who died. Convalescing troops were accommodated in tents on the lawn when King George V and Queen Mary visited on 14 November 1914.

Officers sit in the sun at the rear of the Forest Park Hotel, No 1 New Zealand General Hospital

After the Indian army left for Egypt in 1916, the premises became part of the No. 1 New Zealand Military Hospital until 1919. After major renovations it reverted to its peace time use and was not requisitioned during WW2. The Hayden family sold the property in the 1950's. There were then several changes of ownership over the next two decades.

In the 1970's Mr. Collins owned the hotel as part of his Forest Park Hotel group. During that time Basil Smith, head waiter and long-time village resident, would welcome Harry Secombe, a TV entertainer, who co-owned a film studio at Brock House (Business Centre, Grigg Lane). He would arrive for lunch in his Rolls Royce 'HS 1'.

7. The Holt - Balmer Lawn Hotel

Where the Balmer Lawn Hotel is today was a bungalow; built in the 1870's (*pictured left in 1895*) and later enlarged, called The Holt. It was owned by the Ings family, who also had the tenancy of The Rose and Crown public house (The Huntsman) in Lyndhurst Road. James Wingate married their daughter and took the tenancy of The Holt enlarging it to become The Holt Hotel in 1900.

With the further extensions it was almost its present size when, in October 1914, it was requisitioned for an annex to the Lady Hardinge Indian Military Hospital, at Tile Barn Hill. Ten acres of land was enclosed for additional tented accommodation. King George V and Queen Mary visited on 14 November 1914.

With Indian Troops going to Egypt, in 1916 it was used by the New Zealand No.1 General Hospital until 1919, when it was refurbished with 40 rooms provided with baths, ready to receive guest again.

Balmer Lawn Hotel and hunt in 1910

Charlie Hibbs drove the carriage that conveyed guests to and from the station.

Prince George, Duke of Kent, stayed for a weekend in July 1923 and spent time seeing the New Forest, but his car gave trouble at Lyndhurst. On taking it to the Imperial Garage, they provided him with one from their showroom to use.

Lady Honywood added the hotel to her group in the 1930's. She would visit by landing her aeroplane on nearby ground. Mr. Cass Gilbert, the American architect of the Woolworth Building, died here whilst recuperating from an illness in 1934.

The hotel was again taken over by the military in 1939 and from September 1943 was the H.Q. of the 3rd Division of Canadian Army until April 1944. Immediately prior to D-Day it was the H.Q. for the military controlled area for the assembly and embarkation of troops and materials between the Lymington River and Southampton Water. During planning Generals Eisenhower and Montgomery paid visits to the hotel. Originally the entrance road to the hotel was across the present cricket square and at the road side was a large

hotel sign upon which an army sign writer advertised 'The Duck and Ducklings'. After the war it reverted again to being a hotel.

On 19 October 1970, a painter's blowtorch started a fire (*pictured opposite*) which destroyed 60% of the roof, damaging 18 rooms on the second and third floors. The present copper roof was put on as part of the rebuilding.

The hotel manager in 1983 was Andrew Coy and he chaired Dr Derek Browne's 'London Marathon Appeal' committee for funds to purchase the Village Hall land.

He distributed a leaflet to campers in Hollands' Wood advertising the hotel bars, and the chemist and the village grocer, and this eventually led to today's Village Shopping Guide.

Chris Wilson and his family purchased the hotel in 1997 and has made many improvements since. The hotel is reputed to have a resident ghost, a gentleman in a white coat with a stethoscope; he may have started wandering in 1914!

8. Your Christmas Turkey from Egg to Table

Until the 1960's it was possible to watch your Christmas turkey grow. The poultry dealer and fishmonger, Frank Chalk, lived at 'Forest Glade' in Brookley Road. Here, he had a large shed in which he incubated the turkey eggs and hatched the chicks. When ready for the outdoors, they were reared in a paddock (now the Brookley Road car park) and it was here that you could watch the growth of a favoured one.

In December, the turkeys were 'despatched'. Many local men earned welcome seasonal money plucking the birds at Mr. Chalk's shop (now Splish Splash Hair and Parish Council office). Copious amounts of beer were drawn from the barrel to quench the thirst during these evenings.

Chalk's poultry and fish shop in 1910

These free-range turkeys, when plucked and dressed were considerably larger than those bought today and were often too large for the domestic ovens. This was overcome with the co-operation of the village baker.

The coke fired ovens at the Purkess bakery had to be kept going during the Christmas holiday, so staff were required to give attention. The labelled turkeys were deposited, either by Mr. Chalk or his customers, in a large roasting tin with a jam jar for the dripping, on Christmas Eve.

Charlie Burt, the senior baker, oversaw the placing of them in the oven for many years. He would have them perfectly cooked for their owners to collect, after church, on Christmas morning. No charge was made, but Charlie earned some tips.

9. Christmas Celebrations 1927/8

Christmas events for all the members of the village were held at the Morant Hall on Lyndhurst Road in this pre-television era. The first was a concert, on 9 December, by the pupils of Miss Wingate's 'Glenholm School', in Avenue Road. This included dancing and sketches by her younger pupils and musical pieces by her older music pupils.

On 14 December the Southern Railwaymen's Servants Orphanage Ball was organised by the local staff to fund the Children's Home at Woking. Late trains took the revellers home to Southampton, Bournemouth, Wimborne and Lymington.

The Morant Hall, Lyndhurst Road, 1920's

Mothers, babies and toddlers of the Infant Welfare group enjoyed their annual Christmas Treat, on the 20th, with presents distributed from a giant cracker. Meanwhile also that night, at the Foresters' Hall situated on the site of the modern Masonic Hall in Grigg Lane, the Christmas Whist Drive and Dance, attracted 160 players, who were rewarded with prizes of poultry, port, chocolates and cigarettes. Many more later attended for the dancing.

Pupils from the Church Schools, assisted by members of the village drama group, held their concert at the Morant Hall during the evenings of the 22nd and 23rd. 'The Red Riffs' costume party of 24 pupils opened the entertainment, wearing costumes made in their sewing class. Later there was a detective play, written by the headmaster, 'The Case of the Laundry Lady's Teeth'.

During the Church Schools breaking-up party on Friday 23rd presents from a laden Christmas Tree, purchased from the concert fund, were distributed by Fred Waterman in the role of Father Christmas.

At the Parish Church of St. Nicholas, a Carol Service was held on Christmas Night, when the organ was supplemented by an orchestra of local musicians.

A Boxing Day Night Dance was enjoyed by up to 400 villagers dancing to a village orchestra, organised by the Parochial Entertainments Committee, in aid of local charities.

30 December saw some 380 people attending the Annual Spinsters Ball. The decorated hall was lit for the occasion by electric light, produced by a generator. It would be more than a year before mains electricity arrived in the village (*as described over the page*).

The Foresters Hall, centre, Brookley Road on the right (Hayter's Garage) and Fibbards Road at the bottom.

Further whist was played at the Foresters' Hall on New Year's Eve, followed by dancing until midnight.

The St Nicholas Church bell-ringers performed the traditional ringing out of the old year with 'muffled' bells and the ringing in the New with 'Clear' bells which could be heard across Brockenhurst (*see page 21*).

In the afternoon of 3 January 1928, 300 attended the Annual Children's Fancy Dress Ball, for tea and dancing, in aid of the Fenwick Hospital, Lyndhurst.

The Sunday School children also had a party at the school on Wednesday the 4 January, when, after a lavish tea, they received presents.

The following day Brokenhurst Manor Staff Golfing Society held their annual dance for 200 members and guests and danced until 2am.

Life then returned to normal - and a fundraising dance for equipment and materials needed for the Fire Brigade's proposed new fire station, to be run by the Parish Council, was held on Wednesday 11 January.

10. Electricity comes to the Village

Whilst Electricity had been available in towns before 1900 it was not until 1928 that a supply was planned for properties in Brockenhurst. Although discussed during the year, on 13 December the Parish Council was still asking about progress to install the supply.

From a Power Development Company official's attendance at the Parish Council meeting, in February 1929, it was learnt that power would be purchased by the West Hampshire Electricity Company from Southampton Corporation, carried on overhead wires to Ashurst, and then underground through the forest, with overhead wires in the villages.

At this time all electricity was supplied by local firms, often with different voltages, before the creation of nationalised companies such as Southern Electric and the creation of the national grid in 1937.

The first mains in Brockenhurst would be from Balmer Lawn to Tile Barn. The next part of the project would electrify from the Railway crossing to the Forest Park Hotel via Brookley Road, and finally from Lloyds Bank down Wide Lane (Sway Road) to beyond Woodlands Road.

A fixed charge would be made of 8/- (40p) per quarter during the winter half-year and 4/- (20p) during the summer for each room using the light, plus 7d (3p) per unit of current consumed. Later the quarterly rate was reduced to 4/- (20p) and 2/- (10p). The Council still considered the tariff too high.

Many, especially on lower incomes, did not consider the standing charge justified installing electric light in bedrooms, and continued using lamps and candles. In 1945 there were still properties with electricity only downstairs. Candles were 1/- (5p) for 36, and the ironmonger, Frank Jeans, advertised the cost efficiency of using oil lamps and paraffin cookers.

The tariff for power for cookers, etc. was 2d (1p) per unit wired on a separate metered circuit without a quarterly charge.

On Friday, 16 November 16 1929, a 'Switch On' ceremony for the inauguration of the village's electricity supply by the West Hampshire Electricity Company was performed by Mrs. H. A. Alexander, sister of the late Edward Morant, at the Morant Hall.

The availability of electricity brought about competition with the Brockenhurst Gas Company which immediately reduced the cost of gas by 2d (1p) per 'Therm'.

11. The Bailey Benefice (Trust)

From 1891 until he died in 1916, Henry Francis Bailey was living at 'Oak House' now Knightwood Court, on the Rhinefield Road.

Henry is buried in the church yard with the inscription "his bequests to charities and his name will live on the records of the Institutions for the help of sailors and their orphans, incurables and suffering humanity".

In his will he left a legacy to the village under the trusteeship of the Chairman of the Parish Council and the incumbent of the Parish Church 'to distribute money to the poor provided that they keep his grave tidy.' Over the past 100 years over £50,000 has been distributed.

Born in Cambridgeshire in 1831, Henry Bailey's mother died in child birth and his father, a Captain with the East India Company, may have died at sea when he was five years old; this could be why his memorial refers to "sailors and orphans".

By 1851 Henry was a merchant for the East India Company and living with cousins in London whose fathers were also employed by the company and many of their children were born or died at sea. His mother's family were also great seafarers. The East India Company was dissolved in 1874.

Henry never married and left an estate worth £220,000 (today £18m) including a cottage at Blakeney in Norfolk. He left a large legacy to the Cromer RNLI and four lifeboats have since borne his name. The last of these was built at Cowes in 1934 and is now on display at the Cromer museum. This was the lifeboat for Cox'n Henry Blogg the most decorated lifeboat man, and was withdrawn in 1969 having been launched 347 times saving 920 lives.

A plaque to Henry Bailey's memory is on the North wall of St. Nicolas church - and bears the inscription 'a quiet life achieving much good'.

12. The Railway to Lymington

Official Powers to build a railway from Lymington to Brockenhurst were first obtained in 1847 but with difficulties in obtaining the land, were not taken up. In 1856 a new attempt was made by the newly formed Lymington Railway Company. George St. Barbe, a banker whose company's bank is now the Lloyds Lymington branch and Alfred Mew, a brewer, from Newport, Isle of Wight. The original tenants of the 'Foresters' Arms' were also both directors.

Powers allowed a railway from Lymington to a junction with the London and South Western Railway at Latchmoor Pond and a station there on 24.5 acres of forest land. The Mayor of Lymington insisted that the trains should run into Brockenhurst station so discarding the Latchmoor option. The line was inaugurated on 8 May 1858 and a first train ran. Unfortunately later that day an official Board of Trade inspection took place and decided one bridge was unsafe, so the service stopped. It resumed on 12 July 1858 with a service of seven trains running on weekdays with three on Sundays.

About halfway to Lymington one of the first 'halts' on the rail system was Shirley Holms, which consisted of a short platform with no buildings or staff. It wasn't on the timetable and there were no tickets. Residents of Boldre and Sway stopped the train by raising their hands.

Brockenhurst Station staff 1880's

Sea salt, produced using salt pans was to have been the principal commodity to be transported, but this trade was reduced when the salt mines were opened in Cheshire. The line to the newly constructed pier was opened in 1884 with a direct ferry link to the Isle of Wight.

In the Second World War the line was extensively used prior to D-Day, and a group of US Army engineers was sent to strengthen bridges and banking. The last steam train ran in 1967. From 2005, the branch line was promoted as a 'heritage' route using older rail stock. The last 'slam door' (passenger operated) train in Britain ran until 2010, when modern trains were introduced.

13. Julia Margaret Cameron, Pioneer Photographer (1815-1879)

In Brockenhurst's new 'down' side station waiting room, built about 1871, was a collection of framed photographs with the inscription *"This gallery of great men of our age is presented for this room by Mrs. Cameron in grateful memory of this being the spot where she first met one of her sons after a long absence of four years in Ceylon"*. It was dated 11 November 1871.

The story behind these pictures is that in 1860 Mrs. Cameron (*pictured left*) moved to Freshwater on the Isle of Wight, near 'Farringford', the home of the poet Alfred, Lord Tennyson. Her husband was a tea plantation owner in Ceylon (Sri Lanka) and came and went - their house was called 'Dimbola' after one of the plantations. To fill her time, Mrs Cameron's daughter gave her a camera to have a 'hobby'; the lady made very good use of it. She installed a studio in a chicken shed, and a darkroom in the home, and soon had a steady stream of callers to have their portrait taken, not least many visitors to her illustrious neighbour.

Robert Browning, Tennyson himself, Charles Darwin, Charles Dodson (Lewis Carroll), Alice Liddel, the muse for Alice in Wonderland, and Ellen Terry, 'the' Shakespearian actress of the age, were among the subjects who sat for her.

Alice Liddell - pictured in 1872

Julia Margaret Cameron regularly used the ferry and branch line from Yarmouth and Lymington. It is believed that the gift of pictures to Brockenhurst Station resulted from the kindness of station staff. Her son's 1871 train from London was delayed in bad weather, and Mrs Cameron, who had crossed from the Isle of Wight to meet him, was taken care of by staff who made sure she was warm and provided hot cups of tea. She gifted the pictures to say thank-you.

The Southern Railway removed the originals to Waterloo in 1936, for 'safe keeping'. They were replaced with copies which remain on display in the booking hall. Other of her photographs are in the Victoria and Albert Museum. Unfortunately despite the offer of 'safe keeping' in London, the originals gifted to Brockenhurst Station vanished. Today each of the ten could be worth up to £100,000!

14. Marlpool House (The Lamb Inn) and Black Bridge

On the Lymington Road opposite Church Lane is 'Marlpool House', so named because of the marl clay excavated from adjoining land. It was originally built in around 1750 as the Lamb Inn.

In 1750 the land was bequeathed by one Thomas Yates and by 1780 it belonged to Thomas Gale. In 1784 it is recorded that 'Thomas Gale, yeoman of Brockenhurst, left 17 acres of land, the income from which was to be used for the distribution of beef and bread for the poor'.

Marlpool House, c1980
(by K. Donaldson)

His will stated that his estate should pay for sixty loaves of bread, valued at one shilling each, to be placed on the coffin. After being set down at the cross, the bread was to be distributed to the poor. Further, a distribution was to be made on the anniversary of his death, 27 March, by the Church Wardens and the Overseers (of the poor).

In March 1931 a question was raised at the Parish Council about the trust, but it appeared that it had gone out of existence with records apparently lost after a distribution in 1830.

In 1817 Rev. Comyn recorded in his informal 'census' that there was a Robert Prescott living at the Inn with four children and a servant but no mention of a wife.

After the inn closed the front shown in the picture was put on but it was removed in the late 1900's when shrubs were found to be growing into the façade, and it was replaced with the present more modern exterior.

Adjoining the Marlpool House property is Marlpool Field, known today as 'Black Bridge Field'. That name derives from the soot covered railway bridge at the end of East Bank Road under which the locomotives stopped prior to platforms being extended in 1936. In the field it can be seen that a considerable amount of marl was extracted. Further up the hill at Tile Barn Farm was a brick yard

Across Black Bridge is a footpath, an old one, used by the Weirs inhabitants to walk to the St Nicholas Parish Church. They would cross Culverley Green (the Common) and between the fields later developed into Avenue and Partridge Roads, and later, from 1846, over the bridge to the Lymington Road.

In 1940 two dug-outs were built for gun emplacements in preparation for any possible invasion, the outline of one can be seen by the path. When constructed there was a clear view of the road up to Tile Barn hill.

Marlpool House was used as a hostel for Portsmouth School Boys, evacuated in 1939, and later as the New Forest Conservative Party's constituency office. Frank Perkins, previously mentioned for unveiling the War Memorial, was secretary to the New Forest's Conservative Party Agent for many years and worked here, a familiar sight walking on his one leg from Partridge Road, and across the station bridges to his office. It is now privately owned.

15. When the School was the Community Hub.

When the Sway Road school opened on 27 April 1863 the building mainly was one long room, which could be divided with curtains.

At that time the school was the only place in the village where any form of public gathering could take place. As more citizens became enfranchised it became the place to hold the annual Vestry and political election meetings.

The 1863 school with the 1888 extension

In 1877 polling took place here for the election of Verderers, when over 600 residents cast a vote. Initially a platform was provided for these occasions but, in 1893, the report of Her Majesty's Inspectors stated that this was not permissible as a permanent addition to the schoolroom. The school was always used as the village polling station from 1894 until the Village Hall was built.

The school was also was the place where local 'Hops', sales of work, and concerts were held. In December 1899, the Brockenhurst Choral Society gave a concert in aid of the Soldiers and Sailors Families Association, connected with the Transvaal War Fund. Small afternoon church meetings, such as the Mothers' Meeting (Union), required the school to close early until, in 1910, the Rev. Arthur Chambers obtained an ex-Army hut as a Church Room to be erected in the playground. This was rebuilt in September 1932. Church services were held here when the Parish church was refurbished.

Community meetings continued at the school until the 1920's when the Foresters' Hall was built in Brookley Road.

16. The Bakehouse

This shop in Brookley Road was one of the last three built in 1912 and became 'Armstrong's Dairy' (*pictured below in 1915*) in connection with Brookley Farm. The farmer was possibly a member of the family who previously had Armstrong Farm on Burley Road.

Those managing the shop included Miss E. Pool in 1918 followed by Mr F.J. Weston from early 1920's until 1930. He also acted as an agent for Jackman & Masters, Estate Agents in Lymington.

Mr. B.A. King was the proprietor for a short duration until, in 1932, Mr. Jorgensen became the farmer at Brookley Farm and had the shop. His daughter was a school teacher but after the war she ran the shop introducing a select range of groceries.

In 1963 the shop was acquired by Jose and Sons, bakers at New Milton. It traded at 'Home Bake' and Mrs. May who had had a business selling bread and cakes at 60 Brookley Road became the manageress.

On being refitted in 1978 the trading name changed first to 'New Forest Bakeries' but later to 'The Granary'.

After further modernization in 2003 it adopted the present name of 'Bakehouse'. It is still managed by the Jose family after 70 years; now by the fifth generation. The shop received the 'Best Bakery' award in Hampshire, in 2014, 2019 and 2020.

17. The Bells of St. Nicholas

'We hear them a calling,

A calling, for us to walk up the hill.'

The original St Nicholas church tower had three bells installed in 1637, 1712 and 1714. These had been cast by Clement Tozier of Salisbury and were hung on a wooden frame. In 1758 the tower was 'presented as decayed' and was taken down and rebuilt with the addition of a spire. This was completed in 1763.

The senior choir members and bell ringers had an annual supper held at the Rose & Crown (Huntsman). In 1923 Fred Waterman revealed that he had attended similar functions for the last 58 years.

In 1924 the frame supporting the bells was in a dangerous condition

St Nicholas church bells waiting to be rehung in 1924

and the tenor bell was cracked. The bells were re-hung and three more were added. The first six bell peal, in 1927, was of 5,760 changes of Grandsire Doubles. It took the local ringers three hours. The late Jack Hull, 16 at the time, rang the tenor. In 1979, 52 years later, Jack rang the treble in the first peal of Grandsire Triples rung on the new bells (*described below*). At the time Brockenhurst was one of the few towers in the Diocese with lady ringers and probably the largest number.

In the 1930's the Brockenhurst Bulletin regularly mentioned the bell ringers, their visitors and other local towers they visited.

The bells were silent from 1940 until the threat of invasion was passed. In 1945, Mr. R.E. Tiller, the school Headmaster, with Jack Hull's assistance, taught a number of teenage ringers. In April 1947 a quarter peal was rung by under 16's to celebrate the 21st birthday of Princess Elizabeth (HM the Queen). It was conducted by Myra Tiller at evensong on the Sunday nearest her birthday. In those years Rev. Haslem would entertain the young bell ringers, after ringing in the New Year with magic tricks while they enjoyed coffee and mince pies.

The bells are light weight, the tenor only being 4cwt and 40lbs. They were, until 1979 when two more were added, the lightest ring of six in the country. This resulted in visiting ringers wanting to add Brockenhurst to their list of 'rung' towers. The eight bells now form a complete octave 'B' flat, and guides say; ' the wood panelled space is quite tight with just enough room for the eight ringers'.

One new bell was the number four. It was purchased with subscriptions from relatives of the New Zealand soldiers buried in the churchyard and dedicated to their memory. This is the bell tolled on ANZAC Sunday each April, with one ring for each soldier.

On a frosty clear New Year's Eve, is there a better sound than the half-muffled bells ringing out the 'Old,' and the 'clear' bells ringing in the 'New'?

(The muffs are pieces of leather strapped on one side of the bell clapper to produce a dull note with an alternate clear one.)

Lyndhurst Road and the smithy, now the Island Shop. On the right is the pound and site of the stocks. 1890's. *See page 7.*

Another view of the smithy, with the Foresters public house behind. Also pictured is Mrs Lovell's coach from the Hinchelsea Estate. 1906.